Hippolytes moth[er was an]
Amazon -
Phedre wants her STEPSON
Phaedre is driven by jealousy -
an outside emotion for which
she is not responsible
has uncontrollable passion.

17th century. Born 1639 - Europe
was engaged in Religious.
convolutions Bloodbaths between
the religious groups.

Phaedre drives Hippolytes to his
death. as well as her nurse

Racine was a Jansenist. opposed
to the Roman Catholic Church.
The Jansenist hated the Theatre *
FRANCE WAS SEEN as a land
of elegance "La femme de quarrel"
his woman who quarrel -

* because they thought it would
corrupt people As it was sexual
Racine created entertainment &
instructive.
incestuous. Phraysians.
Phaedre was jealous of Hippolyte
who was virginal & devoted to Diana
the goddess of purity.

The only reason to kill someone
would be treason or lack of
fealty.
Aunt of — us Common mother of
Hippolytus. Theseus

The 17th century was on the
verge of moral collapse
r Racine perceives the
breakdown of society.
L'Homme Moyen = a man who
sees nothing.
There was no moral imperative
abandons Ariadne for Phaedra.

Phaedra feels it is precise to
marry a step-son although it
is not against the law.
In ancient times. Royalty could
not be left alone. -
In medieval times the dogma was
seen as a corrupter - of Gods.
Phaedre is so misled she cannot believe
that there is a rival (Aricia)
Hippolytus is fragmented -

agapé : giving love w/o possession
eros - lust/diabolical.
peripetea - reversal of fortune

PHÈDRE

JEAN RACINE

PHÈDRE ≈ 1677.

A NEW TRANSLATION BY

TED HUGHES

FARRAR, STRAUS AND GIROUX

NEW YORK

Farrar, Straus and Giroux
19 Union Square West, New York 10003

Printed in the United States of America
First published in the United Kingdom in 1998
by Faber and Faber Ltd, London
First American edition, 1999

Library of Congress catalog card number: 98-74825

PHÈDRE, *Queen of Athens*
THESEUS, *King of Athens, Phèdre's husband*
HIPPOLYTUS, *son of Theseus and Antiope, an Amazon*
ARICIA, *granddaughter of Erechtheus, once the King of Athens*
OENONE, *Phèdre's nurse and retainer*
THÉRAMÈNE, *Hippolytus's friend and counsellor*
ISMÈNE, *Aricia's attendant*
PANOPE, *citizen of Troezen*

Phèdre was first performed in this version by the Almeida Theatre Company in Malvern, England, on August 6, 1998, with the production opening at the Albery Theatre, London, on September 3, 1998, and traveling to the Brooklyn Academy of Music in New York in January 1999. The director was Jonathan Kent, and the cast:

PHÈDRE *Diana Rigg*
THESEUS *Julian Glover*
HIPPOLYTUS *Toby Stephens*
ARICIA *Joanna Roth*
OENONE *Barbara Jefford*
THÉRAMÈNE *David Bradley*
ISMÈNE *Avril Elgar*
PANOPE *Holly de Jong*

PHÈDRE

ACT I

(Hippolytus, Théramène.)

HIPPOLYTUS

I have made my decision.
It is six months now
And there hasn't been one word of my father.
Somebody somewhere knows what's happened to him.

Life here in Troezen is extremely pleasant
But I can't hang around doing nothing
With this uncertainty. My idleness makes me sweat.
I must find my father.

THÉRAMÈNE

But where, my lord, would you begin to look?
We have done all we can to find him.
Our ships have searched both seas, they have gone
As far as the Acheron
Where it dives to the underworld, and nowhere
Can Theseus be found.
We have searched Elis, and on past Tenaros,
As far as the ocean
That drowned Icarus when he fell out of heaven.
We have searched every coast within reach
For news of the King and found nothing.
Do you think you'll fare better?

What unsearched patch of the earth do you think might
    hold him?
In any case, who knows—
He might have chosen to vanish.
He might be lying low for his own good reasons.
Perhaps while we rack ourselves
Imagining his death,
He is lolling at ease, tucked away
With some beauty—soon to be deserted.

HIPPOLYTUS

Théramène, Theseus is our King.
He is also my father.
His youthful follies are over.
Phèdre need no longer fear a rival.
Nothing of that kind can have detained him.
But this is now my duty: to find him.
I cannot stay here. Anyway, I dare not.

THÉRAMÈNE

Dare not?
Stay here—in your childhood sanctuary?
As long as I have known you
You have preferred this house,
These gardens and woods and these hills,
To the pompous tedium of the court
And the din of Athens.
What can have occurred in this household
To make you fear it?

HIPPOLYTUS

Everything has changed since the gods
Decided to grace this palace
With the daughter of Minos and Pasiphae.

THÉRAMÈNE

I understand. The world is not blind.
Your problem is real. It is Phèdre.
She persecutes you and she spoils your life.
Your stepmother!
Yes, a diabolical woman!
She had hardly set eyes on you
When she had you removed—right out of the country.
But is her hatred still so virulent?
Is it what it was?
Besides—what could you fear from her?
A dying woman, wanting only to die,
Sick with some sickness of which she will say nothing,
Tired of herself, tired of the very daylight!
How could she plot anything against you?

HIPPOLYTUS

Phèdre's futile hatred of me
Is something I never feared. Théramène,
What drives me away from this house
Is a peril of another order.
The girl Aricia! The surviving daughter
Of that family sworn to eliminate ours.
I have to get away from Aricia!

THÉRAMÈNE

What?
You can think that girl your enemy?
What if she does belong
To the venomous lineage of Pallas—
She never shared their guilt, not one spot of it.
She is utterly innocent. And such a beauty!
How can you hate her?

HIPPOLYTUS

If hate were what I felt, would I run from her?

THÉRAMÈNE

My lord—
How am I to understand you?
Is this the man I know?
Is this Hippolytus?
Our Prince of Scorn, who laughed at love and lovers?
Who mocked the yoke that time and again
Bent your father's neck and brought him down
On all fours, like any common man?
Maybe Venus
Has suffered your taunts
A day too long?
Maybe she now vindicates your father.
Has she forced you,
Even you,
To kneel at her altar
Bending your neck—
Hapless, her sacrificial victim?
Is she bringing the groans out of you?
Are you in love?

HIPPOLYTUS

My dear old friend,
From the first breath I drew you have known me.
You know my pride. It is inborn.
Do you think I could renounce it?
It is no small thing.
I drank this spirit in with my milk
From the breast of an Amazon.
And when I grew up
I exulted to find it in me, like a strength.
You remember, in my boyhood,
When you told me stories about my father,
How I devoured your voice.
My whole body blazed when you described him
Filling the empty place of Hercules.

Monsters slaughtered, bandits rooted out,
Procrustes, Cercyon, Sciron, Sinis,
The giant's bones littered through Epidaurus,
Crete reeking with the blood of the Minotaur.
But when you came to his lighter conquests—remember
How little I liked it?
All those false vows given, and all swallowed!
Periboea's tears at Salamis,
Helen stolen out of her bed in Sparta—
So many, he has forgotten their names.
Ariadne wailing under a cliff,
Phèdre kidnapped—though she became his wife.
Recall how I begged you to be brief?
I would have been happy
To see rased from the memory of mankind
That half of his record.
And now you think I could follow him
Into that kind of dishonour?
You think the gods
Could do that to me?
If I went that way
My sighs would be more than pathetic,
They would be contemptible.
Theseus
Has amassed huge wealth
In superhuman feats and trophies and triumphs
To excuse his occasional foible.
My story contains not one monster.
My only wealth is my pride,
Which leaves me no leeway for folly.
But even if I had to succumb
Would I have picked Aricia?
Do you think I am unaware
Of the gulf between that girl and me?
My father has condemned her never to marry.
He fears a shoot from that unruly stock.

He will bury their lineage with their sister,
Keeping it under guard until she dies.
Do you think I am mad enough
To take this girl's part against my father?
Defy such a man as my father?
Make my name
A synonym for—imbecility?
To launch my life with that doomed enterprise?

THÉRAMÈNE

My lord, once love has picked its man
The gods cancel all his protestations.
Theseus, trying to seal Aricia
From the eyes of every man,
Opened yours.
Theseus' hatred for Aricia
Surprised in you the opposite emotion.
Aricia
Has become irresistible—to you.
But why shy from this passion?
If you feel it—embrace it.
Why forever tangle yourself, my lord,
In these timid scruples?
Hercules never hesitated.
No heart ever begrudged the touch of Venus.
You reject love
But where would Hippolytus be
If Antiope, your indomitable mother,
Had not nursed that flame for your father?
In any case,
This pride which has given you such a name,
What does it amount to?
Admit it, things have changed.
You are not seen much lately, my lord,
Unperturbed, untouched, untouchable,

Hurtling along the sands in your chariot.
Or imitating the god of the ocean
Breaking a wild horse to amuse yourself.
And why are you heard so rarely these days
Scouring the woods with your hounds?
In your eye there's a new kind of fire—
Secretive, heavy, like an ailment.
You try to hide it. But it is killing you.
There is no hiding it. You are in love.
Is this Aricia?

HIPPOLYTUS

I am going. The King must be found.

THÉRAMÈNE

Will you see Phèdre before you leave?

HIPPOLYTUS

Since it is my duty I cannot avoid it.
But here comes Oenone. Something has happened.

(Enter Oenone.)

OENONE

My lord, I can't think how I can bear it.
The Queen is slipping away. She cannot last.
Day and night I watch her, but it's no use,
She is dying of some disease she hides from me.
Her soul is in turmoil. Her entire body
Is convulsed with anguish. She flings out of her bed
Desperate to see the day
At the same time she orders me
To shut the whole world from her sight.
Her suffering frightens me. She is coming.

HIPPOLYTUS

And I am going. At the very least
I will spare her the sight of a face she hates.

(Exeunt Hippolytus and Théramène. Enter Phèdre.)

PHÈDRE

No further, Oenone. I stop here.
That last scrap of strength has left me suddenly.
The sun's light is too painful.
My wretched, trembling legs cannot support me.

OENONE

O you gods, look at her tears!

PHÈDRE

What a useless weight, all these jewels!
And these veils! Whose interfering fingers
Twisted up my hair in these knots?
Everything conspires to torment me.

OENONE

No matter what you say, you contradict it.
One minute ago you ordered us
To braid and set those coils exactly so.
And it was you, madam,
Gathering all your strength, made the decision
To face this splendid sun and the world.
And now at your first glimpse of it you recoil.
How can you fear the sun you longed to feel?

PHÈDRE

You brilliant founder of a benighted family,
You whom my mother dared to call her father,
Maybe you blush to see me like this.
You god of the sun—look at me for the last time.

OENONE

This longing for death is going to kill us both.
I exhaust myself to keep you alive
When all you are doing is trying to die.

PHÈDRE

I want to be hidden in a dark wood.
I want to see the chariot go bounding past
In a fearless cloud of dust.

OENONE

What do you mean?

PHÈDRE

Where am I? What am I saying?
Where did those words come from? My mind is strange.
Some god has taken my senses.
My face feels to be coming apart
With all the turmoil. Oenone!
I can't hide it—everybody
Stares into my shame and its secret.
I can't control this weeping.

OENONE

If you have to weep—then weep
For the way you are stifling what you suffer
Which makes it all the more violent.
You reject our care, our advice.
Do you intend to die in this fashion?
What kind of perversity
Cuts off your days halfway? Is it witchcraft
Shrivelling the springs of life? Is it poison?
Three whole days and three whole nights
You have not slept or broken your fast.
What right have you to throw away your life?
You insult the gods who gave it to you.

And you betray the oath you gave your husband.
Also remember your children.
What will your death mean for their future?
The day their mother dies—
The same day brings new hope
To the son of the foreign woman.
That born enemy of your blood.
That boy from the womb of an Amazon—
Hippolytus.

PHÈDRE

Aaagh!

OENONE

Now I have touched you.

PHÈDRE

The name! You spoke that name!

OENONE

Yes, let your rage blaze out. Curse that name!
I am glad to see you shudder at it.
Live. Renew yourself
With love, with duty. Live—
If only to prevent this sprig of a Scythian
From crushing your sons and all the noble blood
Of Greece, and the gods, under his arrogant throne.

Hurry!
Every moment takes a little life.
You have damaged your strength. You can repair it.
Your flame has burned low, but it burns.
It will grow if you will nourish it.

PHÈDRE

I have lived too guilty for too long.

OENONE

Guilty of what? What is all this remorse?
What crime could be so awful?
You never stained your hands in innocent blood.

PHÈDRE

I thank heaven, my hands are clean enough.
I wish to God my heart resembled them.

OENONE

I think you have plotted something dreadful—
Something so evil you have frightened yourself.
What is it?

PHÈDRE

I have said too much. Let us leave it.
Let me die before I do something worse.

OENONE

Then die—and take your monstrous secret with you.
But find somebody else to close your eyes.
Your flame may have shrunk to next to nothing
But mine will be out before it.
Among the thousand roads to the land of the dead
Mine will be the shortest and the quickest.
Madam, when did I ever betray your trust?
When you dropped from the womb my arms caught you.
You know I gave up everything for you—
Country, children, everything. And now
You repay my loyalty with this.

PHÈDRE

What do you hope to gain by such anger?
If I were to say what I could say
You would be struck dumb.

OENONE

What could be worse than standing here
Helpless—watching you kill yourself.

PHÈDRE

When you know my crime, when you know
The fate that has broken me,
My death will be no lighter. But my guilt
Will be by that much heavier.

OENONE

Madam,
By all the tears I have shed throughout your life,
For your sake, let me know. What is it?

PHÈDRE

Very well.

OENONE

Open your heart. Let me hear it.

PHÈDRE

What can I tell her? Where can I begin?

OENONE

These vague terrors mangle me. Be clear.

PHÈDRE

The curse of Venus is fatal.
What a crazed, pitiful thing
She made of my mother!

OENONE

Madam, forget that. Let the future too
Utterly forget it.

PHÈDRE

Remember Ariadne, my sister.
Her love was like some hideous injury
That killed her on the beach where she lay abandoned.

OENONE

What is it? Why bring all this up?
Your family had bad luck in love.
Why mourn them again?

PHÈDRE

Because Venus demands it. And because
In our whole unfortunate succession
I die last and the most miserable.

OENONE

You are in love?

PHÈDRE

I am in love, yes, I am in love.

OENONE

Who is it?

PHÈDRE

I cannot think of the name steadily.
It fills me with fear to whisper it.
I love—the very name will kill me, I think.
I tremble at it, I shiver—

OENONE

Who?

PHÈDRE

You know him.
That son of the Amazon. That noble prince
I persecuted since the day we met.

OENONE

Hippolytus!

PHÈDRE

You named him.

OENONE

God in heaven!
Ah, my whole body's gone to ice.
What an inheritance!
Yes, your family is pitiable.
Why did we come to this accursèd country?

PHÈDRE

My sickness began much earlier.
That day I married Theseus in Athens,
The moment the ceremony was over,
That moment of the surest happiness
I had ever felt in my life—
Suddenly he was there
Standing in front of me,
He had simply appeared—
Staring at me,
The man created
To destroy me.
Before I could grasp what I'd seen
I felt my face flame crimson—then go numb.
My whole body scorched—then icy sweat.
My eyes went dark.
I could not speak. I could hardly stand.
I knew then the goddess had found me—

The latest in the lineage that she loathes.
I had fallen
Into her furnace—
And I was trapped.
I tried to appease her.
My prayers were incessant.
I built her a shrine.
I spent half my wealth to decorate it.
From dawn to dusk I sacrificed beasts,
Searching their bodies for my sanity.
Futile placebo for a fatal illness!
And the incense I burned—equally futile!
All useless. Whenever I prayed
And bowed down to her image
I saw only his —
I adored only his.
Though I made the air shake with her titles
My whole heart and soul, my whole body
Worshipped only him—Hippolytus!
Then I began to avoid him.
But that was useless too.
I met him everywhere
In the face of his father—
Everywhere I saw him staring at me
Through his father's features.
So then I turned against him.
I turned against myself—to defend myself.
I forced myself
To make his life a misery. At last
I went the whole way—and drove him into exile.

Yes, I played the stepmother.
I pretended to hate him as my stepson.
As if his very presence poisoned me.
Night and day, Theseus had to hear that.
And finally he relented.

So—his own father forced him to go.
Then I could breathe again, Oenone.
Once he'd gone the days flowed past me calmly.

I could conceal my anguish. I could be faithful.
I could even bear children.
But then, of a sudden,
All my precautions came to nothing.
Fate is inescapable.
Theseus brought me to Troezen.
And here, in Troezen,
I had to confront the one I had banished.
The first sight of him ripped my wounds wide open.
No longer a fever in my veins,
Venus has fastened on me like a tiger.
I know my guilt, and it terrifies me.
My own craving fills me with horror.
I detest my life.
I would have preferred to die
With what ought to be hidden cleanly hidden,
And my name intact,
But now you know everything
I will not regret it.
If only you will let me die quietly
And stop lashing me with these pointless reproaches,
And stop making such efforts to keep me alive.

(Enter Panope.)

PANOPE

Madam, against my will I bring bad news.
And you will have to hear it. Forgive me.
Death has taken your husband, Theseus.
The whole world knows of it. Except you.

OENONE

What did you say?

PANOPE

The Queen must now accept that her prayers
For the King's safe return are unavailing.
His son, Prince Hippolytus, has learned
From ships just docked in port: the King is dead.

PHÈDRE

Oh God!

PANOPE

Now the question is: who rules Athens?
The city is divided. Madam,
One side gives its voice to your son.
But the other, ignoring ancient law,
Gives its voice to the son of the foreign woman—
To Hippolytus.
And rumour has it that a turbulent faction
Is determined to crown Aricia,
Heiress to the blood of the Pallantes.
I thought it right to warn you.
Hippolytus is almost aboard.
Once he sets foot among the Athenians
In this broil, with everything so doubtful,
That giddy population will be his.
You would be right to fear it.

OENONE

You have said all that is needed, Panope.
The Queen, you can be sure,
Will not be blind to its significance.

Madam, I had given up all hope.
I meant to go with you
Into the grave. I had not a word left
To restrain you one more hour.
But this news demands a different spirit.
Fortunes have changed and yours is smiling at you.
The King is dead.
Who takes his place?
Your son is the heir.
The King's death leaves you to enforce his claim.
Die—and he's a slave.
Live—and he is a king.
If you die who will support him, or guide him,
Or console him?
You will have betrayed him.
His bitterness
Will be heard in heaven, the gods will hear it.
He has forebears among them
And they will not forgive you.
Live—live! You have nothing to be ashamed of.
Your love is as guiltless as love can be.
Theseus' death has liberated it.
It is no longer criminal and condemned.
Hippolytus becomes accessible—
No longer a man to be feared.
You can meet him freely as you please.
But you must move quickly.
Most likely,
Convinced as he is of your antipathy,
He will mount this coup—to seize Athens.
Madam, undeceive him.
Confuse his decision.
He knows too well that ancient law debars him
From the throne of Athens. Ancient law

Gives that throne to your son and to no other.
Hippolytus inherits
Only the crown of Troezen.
This is his lawful share of Theseus' realm.
Let him have this.
Then you can join with him, madam,
Against the common enemy: you and he
Combine your forces against Aricia.

PHÈDRE

Yes, yes, yes, your words are only too clear.
Now let me live—if that be possible.
Let my love for my son be strong enough
To revive what's left of my spirit.

ACT II

(Aricia, Ismène.)

ARICIA

You say Hippolytus has asked to see me?
It can't be true. You must be mistaken.
You say he's looking for me?

ISMÈNE

To say farewell.
This is the first effect of the King's death.
Prepare yourself.
The hearts that Theseus diverted from you
Will now come flocking back. Aricia
Is queen of her own destiny—at last.
Soon the whole of Greece will be at your feet.

ARICIA

You are sure this isn't a rumour, Ismène?
Am I free? Is my jailer dead?

ISMÈNE

The gods are no longer against you.
The ghost of Theseus has joined your brothers.

ARICIA

How did he die?

ISMÈNE

Accounts conflict.
Mostly incredible. They say
This faithless husband drowned
In some escapade with a woman.
Others go further. They say
He went with his friend Pirithous
Down into the underworld.
If it can be believed
He strolled along the banks of Hell's river
Letting the dead gaze at his living body.
Then found himself trapped in that black land
From which nothing emerges.
All Greece is buzzing with it.

ARICIA

Can you believe that a man before his death
Would visit the land of the dead? Why should he?
What could be the attraction?

ISMÈNE

The King is dead. Nobody doubts that.
Except you. Athens is in mourning.
Troezen confirms his death
By crowning Hippolytus.
Phèdre is frightened for her son.
She has summoned her anxious friends to advise her.

ARICIA

You think Hippolytus will treat me kindlier
Than his father did? A longer chain?
Will he pity me, do you think?

ISMÈNE

Madam, he will.

Haven't you heard? Hippolytus is bronze—
Dangerous and hard, without feeling.
To think he will pity me
And exempt me alone
From the revulsion he feels for all our sex
Ignores the reality. Have you not noticed
The lengths he goes to—simply to avoid me?
How carefully he limits all his movements
To my absence?

ISMÈNE

Of course I know what others say about him,
But I have also watched him in your presence.
That awesome, inflexible hauteur,
The very fame of it, as I observed him,
Doubled my curiosity. Madam,
What I had heard of him and what I saw
Were nothing like each other. Your first glance
Reduced him to total confusion.
I saw he could not take his eyes off you—
He tried to, but he could not. Those eyes, madam,
Were painful with longing—helpless longing.
The name of lover, perhaps, hurts his pride.
His words, maybe, protect his reputation.
But those eyes told everything.

ARICIA

Ismène,
What you say you might have imagined
But I am famished for it, I devour it.
You know my life—
You know how Fate has used me,
Like the toy of a cruel child.
Whatever feeling I had
Was what could survive on grief,

Nourished only by tears.
What can I know about love?
What can I know about the follies,
The luxury, the anguish?
How could I possibly know it?
Among all Erechtheus' descendants
I am the last.
Of all my family, war spared only me.
The sword cut off our name.
It cut off all my brothers.
The earth could hardly stomach so much blood.
You know, too, when Theseus murdered them
He made a law
That no Greek should ever marry me.
Afraid my brothers' ashes might somehow
Blaze into life—out of their sister's womb.
But you know what contempt I felt
For this conqueror's petty vigilance.
Love had never interested me.
My whole life I despised it.
So I could almost thank him for his fears.
He merely officialised my chosen life.
But that—that was before I saw his son.

The whole world admires Hippolytus,
For grace, for beauty.
They are his natural gifts—the more dazzling
For seeming so unconscious.
I was dazzled.
I was even more dazzled
By something richer:
His father's strengths—without the weaknesses.
But what dazzled me most, and I admit it,
Was that pride—that flawless disdain
No woman has ever touched.
The dubious kisses of Theseus

May be the glory of Phèdre.
I set a higher value on myself.
I would be ashamed to cling to favours
Debased and distributed among hundreds.
To be locked up in a heart open to any.
No. But think—
To bring that obdurate spirit to its knees!
To render that unfeeling arrogant soul
Sick with desire.
To see him bound
In bonds he cannot break—
Bonds he only prays to be tighter.
This thrills me. This is what I want.
Hercules was overpowered
Far too easily to bring much credit
To the various women who won him.
Perhaps I am prattling foolishly.
You may hear me regret these words.
More likely he will resist me, or ignore me,
And stay impenetrable.
This hard pride of his that fascinates me
Might yet break me. Hippolytus in love!
What freakish reversal of my fortunes
Could begin to sway—

ISMÈNE
Hear for yourself. He's coming.

(Enter Hippolytus.)

HIPPOLYTUS
Princess, before I leave I should inform you
What has been decided for you.
My father is dead. My fears were not misplaced.
Nothing but death could have imposed on Theseus

Such a protracted silence.
The gods have finally
Given to the fatal three sisters
Hercules' friend, and heir, and sole equal.
You hated him, I know.
And yet I think you will grant him those honours,
And acknowledge his achievements.
I must mourn for my father.
But one thing lightens my grief:
You live a prisoner: I can free you.
I free you: from a law
That has always seemed to me barbarous.
Your life and your heart are now your own.
Do with them as you please.
Troezen has descended to me
Direct from my grandsire Pittheus.
By a unanimous voice, I am now King.
In this kingdom of mine
You are as free, madam, as I am myself.
Or rather, much freer.

ARICIA

Your generosity is too great—too sudden.
More than you can know,
Bestowing so much on my misfortune
You bind me
To the same austere law from which you have freed me.

HIPPOLYTUS

The Athenians cannot decide who shall rule them.
They have named the son of Phèdre. And me. And you.

ARICIA

Me?

For myself I have no illusions.
A Greek law discriminates against me
Because my mother was a foreigner.
Even so, if my only rival
Were the son of Phèdre, my half-brother,
My claim is strong enough. And I could assert it
To push aside that scruple of the law.
But, Princess,
An even stronger claim reins me back
From entering this race. I mean—your claim.
I pass to you, or rather I restore it,
The throne of Athens, which is yours by right—
Descending directly to you
From Erechtheus, the great son of Earth.
Aegeus came to it by adoption.
Athens then confirmed the succession
To Theseus, his son, for his tireless service
Enlarging and defending the city.
Your brothers' claim
Was meanwhile passed over and forgotten.
Now Athens wants you back.
She is sick of this everlasting quarrel.
Too much of your family's blood, for too long,
Has gone smoking into the very soil
That bore your progenitor.
Troezen is mine. Crete and its territories
Are kingdoms rich enough for Phèdre's child.
And Greece is yours. What I shall do now
Is reunite the votes scattered among us
Behind your single name.

ARICIA

Everything you say is astonishing.
It is too like a dream. Is it a dream?
Am I awake? Who could believe this?

Some god has possessed you to think such thoughts.
I see now why the whole world honours you,
And how far you surpass their admiration.
To crown me you will depose yourself!
It was enough simply not to hate me.
Simply to have withheld yourself so long
From that hostility—

HIPPOLYTUS

Me hate you?
My pride, I know, is given hard names
But do you think I came from the womb of a monster?
There is no human temperament so brutal,
No hatred so ossified with habit
That could look at you and not soften,
Not be enchanted, not be captivated.
Could I be the exception?

ARICIA

My lord!

HIPPOLYTUS

No!
Now let me tell you. Now I have begun.
When passion boils, reason evaporates.
I mean—when the heart boils, when love moves.
My secret has become unbearable.
I cannot hold it in any longer.
Am I Hippolytus the arrogant?
Am I a prince? Or a king?
No, I am a beggar—to be pitied.
Not so much the exemplar of pride
As of the stupidity of pride.
I set this lofty pride against love.
I mocked her captives in their ridiculous chains,
I saw her clowns shipwrecked and I laughed

To watch their storms while I sat safe ashore.
But now you see me,
Flotsam in that tide of the common law.
A single surge has swept me far from myself.
A single wave, and it has overwhelmed me.
It happened in a moment.
Now this famous pride is crying for help.
Desperate, humiliated,
With the arrow in me,
Six months of mortification,
Fighting you, fighting myself.
I search your absence for you like a madman,
And yet I run from your presence.
Everywhere in the woods your image hunts me.
I try to escape you
But every shaft of sunlight,
Every night shadow
Sets you in front of me, surrounds me with you.
Everything competes to fling
The obstinate fool Hippolytus
Helpless at your feet.
All my studied care to preserve myself
Has brought me to this—I have lost myself,
I search—but I cannot find myself,
My bow, my spears, my chariot,
They beckon to me, I ignore them.
The breaking and taming of wild horses,
Everything the god of the sea taught me,
It is beyond me—I have forgotten it.
My own horses run wild—
They have forgotten my voice.
Nothing hears my voice but the forest—
The black echoing depth of the forest.
Yes, my love is a savage.
What raving words these are!
Maybe you blush to hear them.

All I had meant to do was declare my love.
Your delicate snare has caught a strange creature.
Princess, grant my words
Perhaps a little more than their face value.
You know this is a language alien to me.
My love speaks crudely, but do not reject it.
Without you, I never could have known it.

(Enter Théramène.)

THÉRAMÈNE

My lord, the Queen is coming.
She's looking for you.

HIPPOLYTUS

For me? Why?

THÉRAMÈNE

She instructed me
That she must speak with you before you go.
I know no more than that.

HIPPOLYTUS

Phèdre! What can I say?
What is she expecting me to say?

ARICIA

My lord, you cannot well refuse to hear her.
As your enemy, it is true,
She is implacable.
But in her state show her a little pity.

HIPPOLYTUS

You must go now. And I shall leave
Uncertain how far I have offended

This beauty I adore,
Or whether the heart I have given you—

Prince, do not delay!
Follow your noble plan and complete it.
Persuade Athens to acknowledge me.
Everything that you have given me—
I accept it. But the throne of Athens,
Glorious and great as it is,
To me is the least precious of your gifts.

(Exeunt Aricia and Ismène.)

HIPPOLYTUS

Old friend, are we all set? Here comes the Queen.
Go, make sure every man is ready
For immediate departure. That done,
Hurry back here and extract me
From a conversation I do not relish.

(Exit Théramène. Enter Phèdre and Oenone.)

PHÈDRE

He is there.
My heart labours. My legs tremble.
I had my words prepared but where are they?

OENONE

Only remember—
You are your son's sole hope.

PHÈDRE

My lord, we hear this sudden emergency
Is removing you from us. I had hoped
We might mourn a little together.

Also, dare I mention it,
I am anxious for my son. He is fatherless
And soon, very soon, he will be bowed
At the grave of his mother.
The boy has few friends,
But, of a sudden, many enemies—
Already moving
To take advantage
Of this moment. My lord,
You are the one man who can defend him.
But you know my fear:
It may be I have turned you against him.
I am afraid
A hatred created by his difficult mother
Will make him its object.

HIPPOLYTUS

Madam,
The very thought of that—I find repugnant.

PHÈDRE

I understand your distaste for me.
It is logical. Inevitable.
You have seen me relentless to hurt you.
But you never looked any deeper.
Yes, I did all I could to provoke in you
A fury of revulsion for me.
I drove you away from wherever I came.
Public or private
In all I said
I was against you.
I set a whole ocean between us.
I made a law that even your name
Should never be pronounced in my presence.
But if the measured penalty for all this
Were truly to match the motive, if your hatred

Answered my hatred and nothing but my hatred,
No woman ever earned more pity
Or less enmity from you than I have.

HIPPOLYTUS

I know that a mother, jealous for her son,
Rarely tolerates the rivalry
Of a half-brother, the son of some other woman.
Seizures of resentment and suspicion
Are expected of a stepmother.
No matter who my father had married
I would have faced the same, and perhaps worse.

PHÈDRE

My lord, God knows, I can swear
Heaven has exonerated me
From that common failing.
A far different passion
Oppresses me, devours me.

HIPPOLYTUS

Madam, our time to mourn has not yet come.
Your husband may be alive.
We weep, but the world might still produce him.
The god of the sea loves him. That great god
Will not have been deaf to his prayers.

PHÈDRE

Nobody goes twice to the underworld.
Once he strayed that far,
If you think some god can extricate him
You are deluded.
Hell never surrenders its prey.
But what am I saying? No—
You are right: he is not dead. I see him.
Theseus is alive. He lives in you.

I look at you and I see him.
My husband's face is this face.
And my love, my need, yes, in spite of myself,
My deprivation, my starvation, my fever—
I can't hide it. He has to know it.
It has to come out.

HIPPOLYTUS

Madam, the abnormal hunger of your love
Projects his image onto other faces.
Though he is dead, his love possesses you.

PHÈDRE

Prince, you are right. I am possessed.
I sicken for Theseus.
But not as the underworld saw him—
The laughing ravisher of a thousand women,
Ready to cuckold even the god of the dead.
Not like that, but loyal and proud,
Even a little diffident perhaps,
Young, and bewitching everybody
With an aura, a magic—
Just as they portray the gods.
Or just as I see you. Yes—
The Theseus I see
Has your bearing, exactly,
Your eyes, your lips,
The very pitch of your voice,
This noble modesty
Gives his cheeks just that flush of colour.
When he came over the sea, to my home in Crete,
The daughters of Minos were besotted—
For a good reason.
Where were you then?
How could he have gathered the flower of Athens
To pay the tribute without Hippolytus?

You were too young! Even so
You could have come with him, on that voyage.
Why didn't you come with him?
To our shores, in that ship?
In spite of all the labyrinth's knots and tangles
You would have slaughtered the Minotaur.
My sister Ariadne
Would have given the thread to you, not to Theseus,
To lead you back to the light
Out of the heart of the monster's riddle.
No, she would not—no, no, she would not—
I would have been there before her
With the plan, and the spool of thread,
To unravel that snarl of dark tunnels
And bring you out of the maze.
Ah, what care and love I could have lavished
On this darling head! Phèdre
Would have come into the labyrinth with you.
She would have come the whole way beside you
To guide you back. Or be killed in there beside you.

HIPPOLYTUS

You gods, what am I hearing?
Have you forgotten that King Theseus
Is my father, and that you are his wife?

PHÈDRE

Can you believe I have lost my memory?
Could I be so reckless with my title?

HIPPOLYTUS

Forgive me, madam. I misinterpreted
Your words about my father.
They confused me. You see, I am blushing.
I am ashamed even to look at you:
I must go—

Now you torture me worse!

Prince, you have understood me perfectly.

I said enough to show you the truth.

Look at me—see a woman in frenzy.

I am in love.

But do not suppose for a second

I think myself guiltless

For loving you as I love you.

I have not

Indulged myself out of empty boredom.

I have not drunk this strychnine day after day

As an idle refreshment.

Wretched victim of a divine vengeance!

I detest myself

More than you can ever detest me.

You are right, the gods are watching me.

Yes, the same gods

Who have filled me with these horrible flames

That are killing me—as they have killed

All the women in my family.

Those sadistic gods

Who amuse themselves, and make their names,

Playing with human hearts.

You know too well how I have treated you.

I not only shunned you.

I acted like a tyrant, I had you banished.

I wanted you to hate me. I wanted you

To regard me as loathsome, inhuman—

Simply to help me to resist you.

All that agony—to no purpose!

Yes, you hated me more. And more and more—

But my love never lessened.

Your sufferings made your beauty more painful.

I writhed, I was consumed

In burnings and tears—

You only had to look at me to see it.
If you could force yourself to look at me.
What am I saying? Oh this is shameful.
Shameful confession! Shameful!
It's you—I have to speak.
You are crushing it out of me.
I came here with a simple small request:
Fearful for my son who depends on me,
I meant to beg you, Prince, not to hate him.
But see how I flung it aside!
My mania burst out, I cannot stop it!
O Prince, I cannot speak to you
Of anything but you. Avenge yourself.
I am depraved. Act. Punish me.
Prove yourself the son of your father—
Rid the world of a monster!
The widow of King Theseus has dared
To fall in love with his son, Hippolytus.
This disgusting pest should be killed.
Look—my heart. Here.
Bury your sword here.
This heart is utterly corrupt.
It cannot wait to expiate its evil.
I feel it lifting to meet your stroke. Strike!
Or am I beneath your contempt?
Maybe my death seems too light a sentence.
Or are you apprehensive
That my polluted blood might foul your hand?
If your hands are reluctant, give me your sword.
Give me that sword!

OENONE

What are you doing, madam! Holy God!
Somebody's coming. Don't let them find you here.
Come, quickly, before they see too much.

(Exeunt Phèdre and Oenone. Enter Théramène.)

THÉRAMÈNE

Was that the Queen? What has happened?
Is there more bad news? My lord,
You look half-crazed. Where is your sword?

HIPPOLYTUS

Théramène, we must leave and leave quickly.
I cannot think of myself without horror.
Phèdre—O you mighty gods in heaven,
If there is a hole in your creation
Drop this secret through it.

THÉRAMÈNE

The ship is rigged and ready. But I must tell you
Athens has announced her decision.
Her chieftains and their tribes have given the crown
To your half-brother. Phèdre has triumphed.

HIPPOLYTUS

Phèdre!

THÉRAMÈNE

A delegation from Athens is here.
Waiting to hand the reins of government
Over to Phèdre. Her son will be King.

HIPPOLYTUS

You gods who know her—is this how you reward her?

THÉRAMÈNE

Meanwhile, my lord, there are murmurs
That Theseus is alive. In Epirus—

So it is said. But we have searched for him
In that very place and we—

No matter.
Question everybody. Neglect nothing.
Investigate this rumour. Follow it right back
To its source in Epirus. If it is false
Then it cannot hinder me. Come,
Whatever the cost, I am going to set this crown
On the head it belongs to.

ACT III

(*Phèdre, Oenone.*)

PHÈDRE

Can't I be free of all this regalia?
How can I parade myself now?
Stop insisting.
And stop trying to console me.
You would be better to conceal me.
I have said too much.
This uncontainable obsession
Has stooped to reveal itself.
I have said what nobody alive
Should ever have heard.
Did you see him?
How he stared as I spoke?
Oh God—how he twisted about
Pretending to misunderstand me.
How he strained to be gone?
And that blushing of his—
The humiliation!
Why did you prevent me
When I had the solution there in my grasp?
That sword has a point like a needle.
When I rested it here, just touching my skin,
Here under my breast—
Did he go pale? For me?

Did he snatch the blade out of my hand?
It needed only a push, one little push—
But the mere fact that I'd touched it
Made his own sword horrifying to him.
He was afraid
That what I'd handled
Might profane
His sacred skin.

Madam, enough of this. You must stop
Raking your miseries over.
You are feeding a fire that you should quench.
You are the daughter of Minos—
The grand-daughter of Zeus—
Far more fitting now to turn your mind
To practical matters.
And far wiser too, to forget this boy
Who has proved so unresponsive.
Take up your proper task, and rule your kingdom.

Me? Rule? Me take control
Of a state flying to pieces
When I cannot control myself?
When I have abdicated
The throne of my own being?
When I am occupied by an enemy
That hardly lets me breathe?
When I am all but dead?

Get right away.

Ah!
I cannot remove myself from him.

OENONE

You dared to banish him. Dare to banish yourself.

PHÈDRE

Too late. He knows my whole madness.
Prudence and restraint are out of date.
Like weak prey torn open
I have bared my innermost, hidden pulse
To my killer. And I cannot help it—
In spite of myself, I still cling to a hope.
When my strength failed before
You brought me back to life.
When my soul was shivering at my lips
You restored it, you flattered its misery.
You gave it hope.
You made me think this love was possible.

OENONE

Whether I am guilty or innocent
I cannot tell. Could I have let you die?
But if my intervention vexes you
What about that spoiled brat's contempt?
Can you forget that face? That baleful blank.
That stone, hewn block. He hardly saw you
While you writhed at his feet.
His ferocious pride makes him repellent.
If only Phèdre had my eyes to see him.

PHÈDRE

Oenone, he might not be what we think.
The forests that bred him kept him wild.

Hunting has made him violent and harsh.
He never heard love speak until today.
He was silent because he was stunned.
It could be we have misunderstood him.

OENONE

Remember, an Amazon bore him.

PHÈDRE

Barbaric, maybe, but she must have loved.

OENONE

His hatred for all women is absolute.

PHÈDRE

In that case I need never fear a rival.
It is too late for this kind of discussion.
Serve my madness now, not my reason.
If his heart is walled up against me
We must find some other unguarded spot.
I noticed how the charms of kingship touched him.
Athens excited him. He could not hide it.
His ships were on the leash—ready to dash
Across the seas to pluck the Athenian crown.
Oenone, go now, work on him cleverly.
Dangle the crown until it dazzles him.
Let him understand—it can be his.
And tell him, Phèdre asks no other favour
Than to set that royal jewel on him.
I cede him all my power. I cannot defend it.
And he can teach my son how to command.
Perhaps be like a father to the boy.
I put both mother and son under his ward.
Go to any limit to persuade him.
Words from you will enter where mine cannot.
Be shameless, weep, groan, anything. Describe me

Close to death. Prostrate yourself. Implore him.
I grant you total licence. Oenone, quickly,
You are my only hope. I shall wait
Here till you return with my fate.

(Exit Oenone.)

You great goddess Venus, are you watching?
Are you happy
To see just how far I have fallen?
It is impossible
To humiliate me any further.
Your victory is complete. Your every stroke
Has gone home.
Goddess of pure remorseless cruelty,
If you still seek for fame
Choose a harder target.
Hippolytus mocks you. He laughs at your furies.
He never uttered one prayer at your altar.
Your very name offends him.
He waves it aside like some polluted fly.
Why not choose him?
He pours the same derision
On you as on me. Avenge yourself.
Make him love.

(Enter Oenone.)

Oenone, why are you back so quickly?
Wouldn't he listen? Is he still adamant?

OENONE

Madam,
Now you need your former fortitude.
Forget your great love: you can bury it.

What did he say?

OENONE

I could not find Hippolytus. Madam,
All those rumours, that seemed so certain,
That convinced everybody, have betrayed us.
Do you hear the roar of the people?
They are welcoming their King.
Theseus is coming from the harbour.

PHÈDRE

Theseus is alive?

OENONE

Any moment
He will be here.

PHÈDRE

Oenone, it's finished.
I have confessed
An appetite that is unspeakable.
With a few greedy words
I have stripped my husband of all honour.
He is alive? Let me hear nothing else.

OENONE

Madam—

PHÈDRE

I foresaw all this.
But you—you were blind.
My guilt was unrelenting—
I only wanted to die.
Then your tears came like anaesthesia.
Even this morning

I could have died with honour.
But then I drank your advice.
However I die now, I die in shame.

OENONE

Die? Why must you always talk of dying?

PHÈDRE

What have I done, O God?
My husband is coming. And his son
Hippolytus—still dazed by my outburst.
I shall have to face my enemy.
I shall have to feel his eyes on me—
Observing just what face I show his father.
Noting my loving words—which he spurned.
And my tears—which meant so little to him.
What do you think?
Is he so sensitive to his father's honour
That he will keep hidden at all costs
What I revealed?
How could he do that? How could he stay silent?
How could he rather connive
At the betrayal of his sire and monarch
Than spit out his loathing for me?
In any case
There's no point in him hiding it.
I am not one of those women
Who manage their infidelity
With a polished smile and a stone heart.
I have not forgotten my ravings.
Every gasp is still alive in me.
Even these walls remember them,
These ceilings are saturated with them,
Every room and passage in this palace
Is bursting to shout my secret
And accuse me. The air is quivering with it.

The moment he steps through the door
He will hear it.
Let me die. My one escape
From all this
Is annihilation.
Is it so dreadful to be nothing?
Despair can find death friendly.
But what a bequest for my children!
Descent from Jupiter is their confidence.
How will they lift their heads
Under my degradation?
Under my folly,
My self-immolation?
Ah!
How will their poor minds endure
The revelations about me, all too true?
The tales that every gossip will barb
And stick into them?
I dare not think
How they will live, buried in their mother's shame.

OENONE

They will not escape. I pity both.
No mother's fears were ever more prophetic.
But why create such a catastrophe?
Why mount this great case against yourself:
If you kill yourself, the whole world
Will be certain you did it because you were guilty,
And could not face the man you had deceived.
Who will be happier than Hippolytus
To have your suicide
Validate the story he will tell?
And what will my version of events
Amount to then? My voice will be wafted aside,
Like a feather. I shall have to listen
To his conceited triumphant sneer

While he regales the court with your behaviour.
Better a thunderbolt wipe me off the earth.
But, madam, has your feeling for him changed?
What do you feel? How do you see him now?

PHÈDRE

A monster! He terrifies me.

OENONE

Then why grant him so easy a victory?
You dread what he might say—that is your terror.
Madam—strike first.
Any moment now he can accuse you.
Accuse him first—of the same crime.
Who could contradict you? Everything
Is evidence against him. His own sword—
Which he left in your hand so luckily.
Your present agitation. Your past distress.
Your perpetual grievance—so emphatic
It turned even his own father against him.
The fact you went so far as to have him banished.

PHÈDRE

Me attack him? Perjure myself
To convict a man who is innocent?

OENONE

Say nothing.
All my plan requires is your silence.
I too have to smother a conscience.
I would rather confront death
A thousand times, than perform this.
But since without precarious surgery
Your death is inevitable, to my mind
The cost is meaningless.
Leave it to me to speak to Theseus.

He will go mad, for a while.
But in the end, like a wise horseman,
He'll halt the runaway furies.
He will punish his son, you can be sure,
With nothing more than exile, as before.
When a father judges his own son
He remains a daddy. For all that,
Innocent blood might still have to be spilt
If it threatens your name. They are coming,
I see Theseus.

PHÈDRE

Aye! And Hippolytus!
That arrogant gaze, plain as speech,
Tells me just how hopeless my case is.
Do what you want, Oenone.
I leave everything to your discretion.
I cannot make one move to help myself.

(Enter Theseus, Hippolytus and Théramène.)

THESEUS

After my long ordeal, at last
Fate has let me through
To my Queen's arms—

PHÈDRE

Stop, Theseus.
Do not profane a greeting of such sweetness.
Phèdre is no longer fit to hear it.
The gods, you should know, are jealous of you.
In your long absence they have not spared your wife.
I cannot delight you. I am no longer worthy
Even to approach you.
Your honour, my lord, has been violated.
Nothing is left to me but to hide myself.

(Exeunt Phèdre and Oenone.)

THESEUS

Hippolytus,
This is a strange welcome for your father.

HIPPOLYTUS

Nobody but Phèdre can explain it.
For my part, sir,
I want nothing more to do with her.
And I beg your permission to leave.
You see how this disturbs me. Let me go.
I cannot exist in her proximity.
Let me simply vanish.

THESEUS

You, my son, leave me?

HIPPOLYTUS

I never wanted her. I never sought her.
She was yours. You brought her into this country,
Into Troezen, with Aricia.
Before you left
You charged me, you remember, to protect them.
That duty is now redundant.
And I have squandered enough life in these forests,
Accumulating boars' tusks and antlers.
I cannot believe you would not prefer me
To be out of this nursery,
Facing something more formidable.
Before you were my age
You were the hero of your own epic,
You had emptied the known world
Of monsters and tyrants.
For every pirate of the two seas
You were Nemesis itself.

Wherever you turned, they simply ceased to exist.
To this day
Travellers are safe.
Hercules could rest on your laurels
And leave his work to you, confidently.
While I decayed here—
The unheard-of child of a prodigious father.
Unmentioned in the hymns of adulation
Sung to my heroic mother.
Let me find employment for my strength.
Let me take up your work.
Or let me at least die the kind of death
That will be remembered
And prove to the world that I was your son.

THESEUS

What is happening?
What is it about me
Sends my family reeling from me?
Has that hellish pit done something to me?
Has it made me a pariah?
If it has
You gods that helped me out of it
Should have left me rotting inside it.
My friend Pirithous was responsible.
He let his idiot lust
Get the upper hand of his judgement.
He tried to ravish the consort
Of the tyrant of Epirus.
Witless, rampant, suicidal folly!
And I—out of pure loyalty—
Was rash enough to aid and abet.
Fate was rightly angered—she made us stupid.
The tyrant surprised us—weaponless.
Then I was forced to watch as he flung
My lecherous companion Pirithous

To horrible reptiles, monsters of the swamp,
Which he kept as pets and fed on men.
For me he had a pit, a steep cavern,
Foetid with stench from the underworld.
I lay under the showering dung of bats.
It was a long time
Before the gods remembered me there.
But they did. They let me outwit my guards.
I paused only to pick up a sword
And butcher that King for his scavengers.
Then came hurrying home. And what meets me?
Just when I think I can be happy
With my family,
Just when I feel my soul
Is coming back to itself—
And only wants to feast and sate itself
In gazing at my family, my beloved,
My children—
I see them staring at me horrified.
I see them shuddering as I approach them.
They squirm from my embraces, they back off,
They cannot get away from me fast enough.
I see such fear in their faces
It fills me with horror—at myself.
I would be happier back in that cavern.
What did my wife mean by what she said?
My honour violated? How? Who did it?
If it's true, why am I unavenged?
Greece looked to me to defend it—
Has it given asylum to the culprit?
You say nothing. Can't you say something?
Am I to assume my own son
Is in collusion with an enemy?
Where is Phèdre?
She swamps me with suspicions
Then disappears. Come.

No man on earth could endure this.
And only Phèdre can unravel it.

(Exit Theseus.)

HIPPOLYTUS

My father's words are more than ominous.
I have seen how far the Queen's derangement
Is beyond her control.
When he challenges her what will she do:
Denounce and destroy herself?
God in heaven, what will he make of it?
Love has unbalanced his entire family.
He thinks I am what I was.
But even I hide a passion
That subverts his law.
I am full of sickening premonitions.
Yet innocence has nothing to fear.
Maybe I can soften him a little,
Find the right words to bring him round,
Persuade him to forbearance
For a love he may not like, but cannot change.

ACT IV

(Theseus, Oenone.)

THESEUS

What? What? This is like vandalism.
Such malignity! So light-minded!
The whole thing so carefully designed
To desecrate his own father's honour.
To deface my name? Defile me?
Nothing could do me worse damage.
Shall I never get out of the labyrinth?
Where am I? Which way can I turn?
That he could think it, is inconceivable!
The brutalised audacity of it!
This is how he repays my paternal care.
And to drive the atrocity home
This thug did not reject the use of force.
I recognise that sword.
I gave it to him—for a different purpose.
The bonds of his own blood could not restrain him.
Phèdre has been at fault. Phèdre
Bears some blame. She deferred his exposure
For too long. Too loath to see him punished,
Phèdre's silence has protected him.

Phèdre protected a pitiable father.
She was so distraught to meet the lust
Aroused in Hippolytus by her beauty,
So shamed by his shamelessness, his importunate grossness
My lord, Phèdre was dying. I watched her own fingers
Guide that point to a softness between her ribs.
I saw her resolution. Had I not wrenched
The sword out of her hands nothing could have saved her.
It is my pity for her and for you
Prompts me now to tell you what I know.

THESEUS

I saw it! He went white when I met him.
And when I approached him—
I recognise fear.
To see his face so drawn—that made me wonder.
And his embrace—
It was so stiff and cold it froze mine.
How long has he been possessed by this?
Was it there earlier—in Athens?

OENONE

My lord, recall how Phèdre avoided him.
His prurient attentions drove her mad.

THESEUS

He started it again—here in Troezen?

OENONE

My lord, I have described what I saw.
You must excuse me. I have left the Queen
Alone too long with her dangerous thoughts.
Allow me to withdraw to be near her.

(Exit Oenone. Enter Hippolytus.)

THESEUS

Ha! Here he comes. You gods in heaven,
How nobly he carries himself!
Who would not be deceived—
As I have been?
But isn't it natural—?
The adulterer's gaze has to inveigle us
With that seamless mask of probity.
If only there were a window
Fixed in the face of every blackguard
To show us the heart behind it!

HIPPOLYTUS

My lord, may I ask
What is weighing on you. I am aware
A dark cloud of some sort sits on you.
You know you can trust my discretion.

THESEUS

Trust you? How dare you
Show your impudent face in front of me?
The thunderbolt has spared you too long.
Last of the vermin to be exterminated!
After your ravenous lust
Has sated itself in your father's bed
You dare to confront him?
To bare that despicable face of yours
Within the reach of my weapon?
In this very palace you have despoiled?
You should be away. That would be wise.
You should be under some other heaven.
In some land ignorant of my name

Where nobody knows or could guess
How rabid you are.
Get out. Don't brave me with your lies.
Do not tempt me to the act
That I am reining back with difficulty.
I have enough—
The everlasting shame of such a son
Is enough
Without the last ignominy
Of having put an end to him myself.
That might soil the glory of all I have done.
Get out. Unless you want to die
Among the trash I have swept into ditches.
And make sure that the sun, the blessed sun,
Never again casts your accursèd shadow
On the threshold of this house
Or on the roads to it,
Or anywhere within my territories.
Get out. Now. Get out.

Neptune, O great God of the Oceans,
Remember how I scoured your shores clean
Of every ruffian.
Remember how you swore to reward me.
You promised me one wish. A single wish.
When I lay festering in that putrid dungeon
I didn't trouble you with it. I saved it.
I kept it for my moment of true need.
That moment has come. Grant me my wish.
Now! Avenge a heart-broken father.
Break your wrath on the head of this traitor.
Smash the bones of his effrontery.
Show how a great god can demolish a man.
Let me see the infinite of your favour
In how utterly you annihilate him.

HIPPOLYTUS

Am I to understand—the Queen has accused me?
I cannot speak for horror.
What you are saying is unthinkable.
The horror of it paralyses me.

THESEUS

You assumed that Phèdre, for shame,
Would hide her defilement,
So your assault on her fidelity
Would stay hidden with it.
You made a mistake. Have you forgotten?
You dropped your sword.
In her hand it convicts you.
You made another mistake. You omitted
To kill her—and cut off her voice.

HIPPOLYTUS

Sir, anger forces me to speak.
To stand accused by you, of such an outrage,
Should force me to give you the whole truth.
Yes, I know the truth. But I suppress it.
It touches you too close. My lord,
Consider a son's solicitude
For the father he loves.
That keeps my mouth sealed.
Unless you wish to open an abyss
Under the gulf that is already gaping.
Recall how I have lived, and what I am.
The first steps towards a great crime
Are trivial misdemeanours.
There is a stairway of degrees
To crime, just as to virtue.
Innocence is demure. A single day
Cannot transform a man of loyal conscience
To an incestuous lecher, a hardened killer.

My mother's chastity was her fame.
There's not a drop of dissolute blood in me.
She formed me. Then Pittheus was my teacher.
The wisest, noblest, best man of his day.
I do not wish to boast but, my lord,
Above all other virtues, the one virtue
That I was born to, and have been bred up to,
Is hatred of this crime you charge me with.
My aversion to it is a legend.
Throughout Greece I am famed for just this.
Some say my rigour is so stubborn,
So severe, so blunt, they think it ugly,
Yet God knows the depth of my heart
Is pure as the blue sky! And still I hear you
Call me a hypocrite—

THESEUS

And I repeat it.
I see through your chastity—plain as day.
That frigid pride of yours is precisely
What betrays you.
Your lascivious eyes are locked on Phèdre.
Indifferent to every other woman
You have no trouble ignoring their attractions.

HIPPOLYTUS

Father, it is not so. You compel me
To tell you what I must withhold no longer.
I am in love.
This will anger you, but I must confess it.
I have done one thing you have forbidden.
Your son has submitted his whole being
To the daughter of the Pallantes—Aricia.
I worship Aricia.
Father, I adore her. My inmost soul
Belongs only to Aricia.

THESEUS

You love Aricia? Heaven sees what this is
As clearly as I do. A fairy tale for fools!
You concoct one crime to hide the other.

HIPPOLYTUS

Father, six months, against my will, I have loved her.
I came here to inform you. It is not easy.
What can I say to make you see the truth?
What heaven-shaking oaths do I have to swear
To make you understand you are mistaken?
I swear on the earth, the heavens, on all nature—

THESEUS

Blasphemy is child's play to a liar.
Stop! Spare me the babbling. You insult me.
Your posturing virtue is incredible.

HIPPOLYTUS

Only to you while you believe the lie.
Phèdre knows the truth. I am not guilty.

THESEUS

Ah! Your insolence is intolerable.

HIPPOLYTUS

If I am to be banished—where and when?

THE WORST PUNISHMENT

THESEUS

Beyond Atlas, far out in the Atlantic—
You would still be much too close to me.

HIPPOLYTUS

Once you have branded my name as a felon
Who in the world will befriend me? If Theseus
Casts me out, who dare take me in?

Find friends among men debauched enough
To approve adultery and relish incest.
Thankless, treacherous men, without laws or honour.
The kind who will welcome such as you.

HIPPOLYTUS

Adultery and incest! You are obsessed
With adultery and incest. Shall I say it?
Phèdre had a mother.
Remember Phèdre's mother.
Phèdre bears the blood of a lineage
Far more heavily charged with such crimes
Than mine ever was and you know it.

THESEUS

What? You are mad!
Get out. For the last time—get out.
Must you wait till I'm speechless?
Do you have to be flung out bodily?

(Exit Hippolytus.)

Yes, go, you filth. You will not escape.
Destruction is hurrying towards you.
The god of the oceans
Swore on that river in Hell
To give me satisfaction.
A god of vengeance out of the seas pursues you.
And yet in spite of your nature,
So strangely diseased,
I loved you. My bowels are twisting
With a horrible foreboding.
You forced me to curse you.
How many fathers have known this?

You gods, you see what I suffer.
How did I sire this deformity?

(Enter Phèdre.)

PHÈDRE

My lord, your voice rings through the palace.
I could not help but hear it.
I am terrified. O my lord,
What if your prayers are answered?
Is it too late to save him?
He is your own blood—rescue him!
Your own sacred blood—cherish it
Before it is too late. I beg you
Save me, Theseus,
From having to hear his screams.
Save me from a life
Haunted by the screams of Hippolytus.
Save me
From the everlasting horror
Of having prompted his own father's hand
To destroy him.

THESEUS

No, Phèdre, I have refrained, not easily,
From dipping my hand in my own blood.
Nevertheless, this rapist is doomed.
Immortal hands are already at it.
Neptune's debt to me will avenge you.

PHÈDRE

Neptune's debt? What?
You call on—

Would you prefer the god to ignore me
Like some ordinary creditor?
My plea to him is holy—you should join me.
Recount my son's crime. In all its detail.
Let me hear the full enormity of it.
Shake up my sluggish spirits.
My blood is too torpid.
You do not know one half his perfidy.
He reviles you in particular—
Nothing but lies, he says, comes from your mouth.
He was almost incoherent.
Finally, as a last insult to me,
He dares to pretend
That he has fallen in love with Aricia.
He swears he has given his soul to Aricia.

PHÈDRE

Given his soul?

THESEUS

Another of his lies.
Everything he says is counterfeit.
He lies as he breathes—
To keep himself alive.
But Neptune, our great green god of the ocean,
His judgement will be swift.
And now I am going
To add my prayers to it.

(Exit Theseus.)

PHÈDRE

Can I believe this?
Am I sick? A smouldering
Here, under my ribs—

Trying to burst into hard flames.
This cannot be true.
I rushed here to save his son.
Oenone tried to stop me.
But her arms were powerless
To hold back the guilt that lashed me,
The remorse that dragged me—
I was out of my mind.
How far would I have let myself go?
Maybe, if what Theseus told me
Had not choked me
I would have gone on. I would have confessed.
The truth would have come vomiting out of my mouth.
But now—
Now I know Hippolytus can feel.
Only—he feels nothing for me.
He loves Aricia!
His heart, his soul, everything
Sworn to Aricia!
Oh God, when I howled at his feet—
When he stared at me
With that statue's face
I thought he was impenetrable, proof,
A bronze burnished visor, deflecting
The whole female sex—
Like his reputation. I was wrong.
It was all a front.
The right woman's touch undid his armour.
I thought his eyes were stone—she found tears in them.
Perhaps he is too susceptible to women.
I am the only one he cannot stand!
And I came rushing here to defend him!

(Enter Oenone.)

Oenone, I have learned something.

OENONE

Madam, when you ran out I almost fainted.
You were in such a state.
I feared it might be the end of you.

PHÈDRE

Would you believe it? I have a rival.

OENONE

What?

PHÈDRE

Hippolytus is in love.
Beyond any doubt.
This enemy of mine, so wild and shy,
So alien to subjection,
Who found my entreaty so appalling,
My tears so irritating,
This tiger
That I could never approach without trembling—
He has been tamed. He is humbled.
And now he announces his love.
Aricia has taken possession.

OENONE

Aricia!

PHÈDRE

What now, Oenone?
What new constellations of torment,
Reserved for this moment,
Of a magnitude I never imagined,
Rise for me now?
All I have suffered before this —
The terror, the delirium,
The agonies of craving, the impossible pain

Of that brutal rebuff, the horror of my guilt,
The bottomless degradation,
The loathing of myself, the despair—
All that was no more than the overture
For what is taking hold of me now.
They love each other!
What sort of witchcraft did they use
To delude me?
How long have they loved each other?
Where have they been meeting? How often?
You knew! You knew it! Oenone,
Why did you let me be fooled?
Couldn't you breathe one whisper of their secret?
Wasn't it plain?
Weren't they forever
Running around looking for each other?
Heads together in corners, thinking themselves unnoticed
In plain view of everybody?
Or did they hide it all in the forest?
Ah! They were free!
Heaven was pleased with their innocent affection.
Wherever their love led, they went light-hearted.
For them the days dawned calm.
But for me, rejected by nature,
I dreaded every sunbeam.
I buried myself.
Daylight was a horror to me.
Death was the only god I prayed to.
I waited only for death.
Nothing but gall sustained me, and tears.
Surrounded by spies
I did not even dare
To unburden myself of my grief.
I concealed it.
I sank
Into the horrible secret luxury of it.

My sobbing was soundless.
My weeping was dry.
I trembled with calm.

Their love is futureless. It has come to nothing.
They will never meet again.

Yes, but their love exists.
It exists. And it will last.
I cannot bear to imagine it.
Even this moment, as I speak,
They have not a thought for me,
They are heedless
Of the fury of my love—
It is meaningless to them.
But I have to endure it—
I have to burn in it.
Banishment may separate them
But it cannot injure their love,
Only intensify their million vows
To love each other for ever.
No, it's their happiness—it's their hope
That torments me.
Oenone, I am going mad with jealousy.
Aricia must die.
Theseus must be made to kill her.
No punishment is enough.
She has outdone her criminal brothers.
I'll use every bit of rage in my body
To persuade him to kill her.
Oh God, what am I doing? What am I saying?
I think I'm losing my senses.
Me jealous? Me beg Theseus

To avenge my jealousy? Implore my husband
To remove my rival
From my monstrous passion for his son?
Everything I say makes my hair stand up.
My life is so bloated with my crimes
There's no room for another. I stink
Of incest and deceit. And worse—
My own hands are twitching
To squeeze the life out of that woman,
To empty that innocent blood out of her carcase
And smash her to nothing.
Yet I stand here facing the sun.
The light of heaven, my greatest ancestor,
Is the father and ruler of the gods.
The whole universe is full of my forebears.
Where can I hide?
I cannot hide even in Hell—
My father, Minos, is the judge of the dead.
There, the judgement favours nobody.
He will be stupefied
When I appear before him. His own daughter!
Forced to confess to such crimes,
So different and so many,
Some of them perhaps
Unknown even in Hell.
Father, how will you judge my life?
I see your hand fall from the dark urn
That contains the lots for the common dead.
I see you groping, aghast,
For the just sentence
That you must execute on your own daughter.
O Father, you have to forgive me.
The pitiless goddess
Would not loosen her grip on your family.
I am one more trophy of her vengeance.

My crimes were execrable.
Their shame walks with me like my shadow.
But they brought me no profit—
Not one flicker of gratification.
No, my every step
Carried me deeper into evil fortune.
My whole life has been wretched and ends in torment.

OENONE

Ah, madam, get rid of these thoughts.
You made mistakes, but view them in a new light.
You are in love: that's fate, it cannot be altered.
Destiny cast the spell that leads you spellbound.
Is that such a novelty?
Mankind is frail by nature.
Submit to being mortal. You are mortal.
The creation has laws.
Even the gods, the high Olympian gods,
Who come down so hard on our weakness,
They find passion uncontrollable.

PHÈDRE

What am I hearing?
How dare you go on mixing these drugs?
Will you try to poison me to the last?
Witch. This is how you have destroyed me.
When I tried to crawl out of my life
You won me to stay.
Your reasoning blinded me to my duty.
I shunned Hippolytus. You made me see him.
Can't you see what you've done?
Your evil incriminating mouth
Has ruined his name
And blasted his life.
It will have killed him

If the god fulfils the inhuman prayer
Of a father you have driven mad.
Get away from me.
Leave me to mourn what you have made of me.
And may the heavens
Pay you exactly
What you have earned.
And your punishment
Terrify
Everybody like you.
All those who do as you have done.
Bending their supple speeches to the failings
Of erratic monarchs.
Giving a little push to their inclinations,
Easing their descent into crime.
Vile whisperers!
Sycophants,
The most
Pernicious of the gifts an angered god
Can give to the wearer of the crown.

OENONE

Ah God, I have spent my life to save her.
Have I now been paid as I deserved?

ACT V

(Hippolytus, Aricia, Ismène.)

ARICIA

You have to speak out.
The danger you are in numbs my mind.
Your father loves you.
You cannot let misapprehension craze him
Against you.
Speak, and save yourself from it. Save us.
You are forgetting us.
Are my tears meaningless? Can you accept
Our separation for ever
Without a word? Then go. Leave me hopeless.
But at least, if you must go, save your life.
Save your name, your fame
From this scandal and this preposterous lie.
Though the truth is vile, force him to face it.
Make him reverse the curse. There is still time.
What nicety of honour
Creeps off speechless leaving all the credit
With an unscrupulous liar? Tell your father,
Tell him everything.

HIPPOLYTUS

Ah God, what haven't I said?
You want me to disclose

The shame of his bedchamber
For the mere relief of feeling truthful?
Can I humiliate my own father
And make him laughable? Nobody
Has looked into this secret
Except you and the gods.
See now how I love you. I have shown you
What I tried to hide even from myself.
Aricia, forget you ever heard it.
I opened this to you in confidence.
Never mention it. It's too filthy a business.
It would contaminate your mouth.
But if the gods can be trusted,
If they want justice, they must favour me.
The situation can be left to them,
And I need fear nothing.
Sooner or later Phèdre and her great lie
Must meet their judgement, which is immovable.
Only for this I beg you to be patient.
But for everything else—I have done with patience.

Aricia, your prison
Need no longer hold you. Come with me.
Gather your courage. We can leave together.
Everything about this place is abhorrent.
The very air corrodes honesty.
Your disappearance now will pass unnoticed.
My sudden disgrace and banishment
Has turned the whole palace upside down.
We can use the confusion.
All that you require, I can give you.
Your guards are my men.
Across the sea our allies are powerful.
Argos calls us. Sparta welcomes us.
Our interests are theirs.
Phèdre shall never dethrone you or me.

She shall never build her empire
Out of our absence,
Or give what is ours to her son.
What now? You hold back?
This is the moment and we have to seize it.
Are you wavering?
Aricia! I am resolved.
If I seem to be moving too fast
It is for your sake.
Do you hesitate
To share your escape with a banished man?

ARICIA

I want no other freedom.
To share your fate is the only
Happiness I can imagine.
But if I come
There is one thing lacking between us
Not only to complete my happiness
But also preserve my honour.
If I can escape
From one who has dealt with me
As cruelly as your father has,
I break no code of honour.
Flight from a tyrant is acceptable.
And neither home nor kindred holds me here.
But, my lord, you love me, and my good name—

HIPPOLYTUS

Aricia, your good name is my first care.
Now hear my plan.
Desert your enemies and marry me.
Misfortune has freed us to do what the gods ordain.
We need no one's presence or permission,
No torches or procession.

Outside the gates of the city,
Among the tombs where my family are interred
There stands an ancient shrine.
That place is so holy
No perjurer dare come near it.
Whoever makes an oath in those precincts
And breaks it is instantly punished,
Their death follows quickly.
In that shrine, Aricia, if you will trust me,
We will consecrate together
An everlasting love. Our one witness
Will be the god of the place.
That god can perform
The role of priest and father to us both.
Then I will beseech Diana,
Goddess of chastity, brightest of all the gods,
To sanctify my vows, and to bless us.

ARICIA

Here's the King. Oh go. Oh God,
Go, go. I will stay here to cover you,
And allay his suspicions. Quickly, quickly.
But leave somebody who can guide me
To the place.

(Exit Hippolytus. Enter Theseus.)

THESEUS

You gods, permit me one ray of light.
Let me catch one glimmer of the truth I search for.

ARICIA

Ismène,
Have everything prepared. And be ready.

(Exit Ismène.)

THESEUS

Madam, you change colour. You seem startled.
What was Hippolytus doing here?

ARICIA

Giving me his last goodbye, my lord.

THESEUS

Those eyes of yours have humbled that arrogant stare.
His first sighs of passion—are all your work.

ARICIA

If that is true I shall not deny it.
One thing he has not inherited from you
Is your hatred for me.
He never saw me as a threat to the state.

THESEUS

Of course not. He was too busy
Swearing eternal love.
Do not depend, girl, on that facile mouth.
He has sworn the same to others.

ARICIA

He has?

THESEUS

You should have restrained him.
How can you entertain such a pretender?

ARICIA

And how can you let that rotten libel
Pollute his life—a current like sunlight!
Do you know your own son's heart so little?

Can't you distinguish between good and evil?
The whole world can see what he is.
Must you—his father—be the only one
Blundering about in the dark?
I can't leave him and his name
To the tongues and fangs of vipers.
Stop now: halt your homicidal curse
And beg the gods to forgive you for it.
Has it occurred to you
They may hate you enough to grant it?
Sometimes the gods accept our prayers
Just for the opportunity it gives them
To punish us in full, at our own request.

THESEUS

Enough. You have scolded enough.
You cannot change the nature of his crime.
Love has blinded you to his ugliness.
I have witnesses—impeccable.
I have seen tears that were incorruptible.
And I believe them.

ARICIA

Be careful, my lord. Your hands
May have eradicated many monsters
And never once failed. But let me say:
Not every monster has been accounted for.
There is one monster you have not recognised—
Your son, my lord, forbids me to say more.
He is concerned for you.
And his concern for you must also be mine.
If I told all I know—he too would be injured.
My lord, let me share his reticence.
And rather than be forced by you to break it
Allow me to withdraw.

(Exit Aricia.)

THESEUS

What's in her mind? What is this woman hiding?
She seems to be trying to tell me
Something she dare not tell me. Starting and stopping.
Going straight at it—then dodging past it.
Maybe the pair have put their heads together
To trick me, and lead me by the nose
Into some fresh maze of new clues—
And new darkness. At the same time,
In spite of my determination,
And in spite of my anger,
A voice—
Somewhere, beneath all this, a voice,
A pleading voice, inexplicable:
Pity—surprising and painful.
Oenone has to be questioned again—more thoroughly.
I need to know more about what happened.
Guards, bring Oenone. Here, alone.

(Enter Panope.)

PANOPE

I dare not guess what is in Queen Phèdre's mind
But her agitation, my lord,
Puts her life in danger.
If despair can be fatal
And if we can recognise its signs,
I see it in her face. She is white as death.
As for Oenone—everything is too late.
She abandoned Phèdre and ran from the palace.
My lord, she leapt from the cliff-head—
And if that drop to the sea did not kill her
The sea did. Whatever her reasons

The waves that are now pounding her body on the rocks
Have washed them away, beyond recovery.

THESEUS

What?

PANOPE

This death has not quieted the Queen.
Only made her worse—if anything could.
She rushes to her children, like a mother
Seeking her own consolation,
Embracing them and sobbing over them,
But then she thrusts them away, with shrieks of horror,
As if maternal love were some contagion,
And staggers about the palace,
Falling on the stairs, colliding with walls
Like a blind madwoman.
She stares at everybody and sees nobody.
Three times she started a letter—
Each time changed her mind and tore it up.
You must see her, my lord. And perhaps help her.

THESEUS

Oh God—Oenone dead?
And Phèdre wanting to die?
Call my son back.
Let me hear my son defend himself.
Let him tell me all he has to tell me.
I will listen. Tell him I will listen.

(Exit Panope.)

O Neptune,
If you heard my prayer, if you heard my curse,

Hear me. Withhold your favour to me.
Perhaps I believed the wrong story,
Perhaps I based my judgement on lies—
Too credulous and too precipitous.
Perhaps my berserk rage, that called on you
To destroy my son, was mistaken!
Oh God, God, if I am too late—

(Enter Théramène.)

Where is Hippolytus? What have you done with him?
I gave him into your care, Théramène,
When he was only a child.
Where is my son?

THÉRAMÈNE

Ah—so much concern
Coming so late and so superfluously.
Such paternal love. And all so useless.
Hippolytus is dead.

THESEUS

Aaah!

THÉRAMÈNE

I have seen
The death of the most lovable of men.
And the most innocent, my lord.

THESEUS

My son dead? Ah! Only now
When I stretch my arms wide open to him
The gods rip him away.
What happened to him? How did they do it?

We were hardly clear of the city gates
And onto the beach road, towards Mycenae.
Hippolytus was leading, in his chariot.
His bodyguards close round him. A sombre troop.
The prince was taciturn.
His mood made the mood of every man.
We all shared one dark thought and were silent.
No sound but the click of hooves and jingle of harness.
Those horses of his were strange.
Usually so bursting with spirits—
So headstrong, so eager to be off,
They need the constant touch of his voice and the reins
To hold them in—today they were listless.
He left the pace to them,
Letting the reins lie loose over their backs.
They hung their heads, they seemed preoccupied,
As if they were helping him, with their hanging heads,
To think what he was thinking.
I noticed it. It seemed very strange.
As I was watching that,
A sudden skull-splitting roar,
An indescribable, terrible, tearing voice,
Like lightning flash and thunderclap together,
Made us all duck and cower.
It came out of the sea, as if the whole sea
Had bellowed.
And then, like an echo to it,
Another roaring groan, subterranean,
As if something that groaned were trying to scream,
Rolled through the earth under our feet.
The ground was bulging, jumping beneath us.
We were petrified and bewildered.
The horses' manes and tails flared on end.
And now I saw out at sea
A mountain of water boiling up,

Heaping higher,
Irrupting from under the horizon
And racing towards us.
Till it towered above us, seeming to hang.
And there, in slow motion,
It collapsed, a solid fall of thunder.
Quaking the bedrock. And out of it,
The foam cascading from a colossal body,
Came a beast—
Up the sand, with the fury
Of a supernatural existence.
Its head was one huge monster all to itself,
Like a bull's head, with bull's horns.
But from the shoulders backwards
The whole body was plated,
Humped and plated, the scales greeny yellow,
A nauseating colour, that sickened the eye.
And beyond the humped bulk of the body
Came scaled and lashing coils. Half bull, half dragon—
Mouth hanging open,
And bellowing, like a heavy surf
Exploding in a cavern.
The earth trembled, the air was thick with horror.
We breathed a mist of horror.
Weapons or courage were out of the question.
Everybody fled. We all took cover
In that small temple among the tombs.
Then I looked back and saw Hippolytus—
He was lashing his horses and making a run
Straight at the monster—at the last moment
I saw him swerve
Tight past its jaws and bury a javelin
All but for a span length of the shaft
Behind that thing's shoulder, right where the heart is
In creatures that have hearts.
I never saw anything so fearless.

But whether the javelin blade found a heart,
Or the beast was convulsed
With fury at his daring—the whole mass of it
Rose and collapsed on to Hippolytus,
Like another mountain of ocean,
Or like a giant octopus of water.
I saw horses and chariot
Tossing among foam and tentacles
That dragged back down towards the sea.
But then, a miracle.
The horses were clambering free,
Like a team scrambling across an avalanche.
And I saw Hippolytus braced in the chariot—
Fists bunched and legs wide,
I thought he was getting clear. But a god was watching.
In a surf of churning sand,
A last scything swipe of the monster's tail
Came round under their hooves,
Toppled the horses and smashed the wheels of the chariot.
Then the horses went mad—
I heard Hippolytus shouting among the screams
Of the horses, and the blasts of that beast.
The wonderful strength of Hippolytus was helpless.
Some of the others saw something
I can hardly credit, I did not see it.
They saw the glowing figure of a naked god
Astride the shoulders of the demented horses—
Goading and urging them
Among the rocks of the foreshore
With the chariot, stripped of its wheels,
Bounding like a bucket behind them.
Hippolytus had wound his arms in the reins.
He tore the horses' mouths but they felt nothing.
And the voice they had grown up with
Became a scream that added to their terror
As the chariot disintegrated beneath him.

Then it was two mad horses dragging a man.
Oh my lord, forgive me! The sight of it
Is like a great wound through my body,
It's never going to heal.
The horses galloped away with their weightless bundle
That had fed them, and that was your son.
We followed—all of us crying openly
Like forsaken children.
The trail was easy—he had signed every stone,
Left us a rag of flesh on every thorn.
The horses careered in a wide circle—
Till they were exhausted.
They came to a halt, as it happened,
Among the royal tombs. There we found them,
Streaming with lather and shuddering,
The eyes crazed in their heads. And there he lay.
It is part of the marvel of his strength
That he was still alive. When I clasped his hand
And called to him, his fingers squeezed my fingers.
His eyes opened—they stared past me awhile
At something he tried to recognise.
Then closed slowly. They did not open again.
He was trying to speak. I bent close.
'The gods have taken my life,' he whispered,
'Though it was innocent. Dear old friend,' he said,
'After my death protect Aricia.
And if my father ever frees himself
From his delusion, and feels any remorse
For that false charge which has destroyed his son,
Ask him to treat Aricia kindly.
Ask him to give back to her—' My lord,
With those words
His voice and his life failed together.
And I was left embracing the latest prize
Of the triumphant gods—an object

Hardly recognisable as a man.
I think his own father would not know him.

My son! I did it to myself—
Killed my only hope. Inexorable—
That is the word for the gods.
They kept their word too well.
Nothing is left to me now, but to mourn.

THÉRAMÈNE

There is a little more to tell you.
Aricia came running towards us.
My lord, she was running away from you,
And hurrying to meet Hippolytus
At that very temple, there, among the tombs,
Where they had planned a marriage solemnised
Only by the god. As she came near
She saw the horses steaming and shivering
In their broken traces. Then she saw
What we stood around and looked down at.
The drained rag of Hippolytus' body.
For a moment she could not recognise
That this was all that remained of her happiness.
Her eyes refused to understand it.
She stared at the corpse and asked for Hippolytus.
But then it sank in.
And she let it happen.
She cried out just once, then dropped, silent,
Like somebody jabbed through the heart.
Ismène was with her.
She managed to bring her round. Aricia
Returned to what was waiting for her—
Daylight, that mangled shape, her future.
And I have come, my lord,

Hating what I have to reveal
And to discharge the task allotted to me
By the dying breath of Hippolytus.
I pass his last wishes to you.
And here comes the cause of everything—

(Enter Phèdre.)

THESEUS

Now you can be happy. My son is dead.
I cannot help it, these vile fantasies
Overwhelm me—though I lack evidence.
I have only one fact—my son is dead.
Madam, he is your victim, rejoice.
Whether guilty or innocent
He can no longer aggrieve you. Accept it.
I am ready to look no deeper.
If you accuse him, let me live with that.
I will think him a criminal and a traitor.
His death alone is suffering enough
Without me searching for scraps and broken bits
Of information that could drive me mad
But never bring him back.
Let me get away from this land
That holds you
And the dismembered body of my boy.
Even if I found another universe
This memory would be with me.
Everything proclaims what I have done.
My very fame blazes with my shame.
If I were unknown I could hide.
The favour of the gods terrifies me—
I dare not ever again pray to them.
Their answers to my prayers have finished me.
However much they have helped me in the past

They have taken everything back, they have taken my son—
My son, my hope, my life.

No, Theseus. Now hear me speak.
Let me restore your son's lost innocence.
Hippolytus was not guilty.

THESEUS

My son was not guilty? So simple.
And it was on your word that I cursed him?
You are Hell itself.
You think this can be forgiven?

PHÈDRE

Listen to me carefully, Theseus.
Every moment now is precious to me.
Hippolytus was chaste. And loyal to you.
I was the monster in this riddle.
I was insane with an incestuous passion,
To amuse some malevolent deity.
That viper Oenone plotted the rest.
Once I had bared my affliction to your son
Oenone feared he might in time inform you
Of my shameless obsession, my shameless attempt
To force my lust on him. While I was helpless
That infernal woman slithered to you
And fixed the guilt on the prince
As if she had witnessed it. So you were poisoned.
She has been punished. She escaped my rage,
And found a gentler executioner
Where the sea breaks under the cliff.
The sword would have been my own choice, before this,
But that would have left the prince's innocence
To the play of suspicion and conjecture.

I have chosen a slower conveyance
To the land of the dead. This has allowed me
Time to show you, Theseus, my remorse.
Now I am drunk on an infallible poison
That my sister Medea brought to Athens.
I feel my pulses pushing it icily
Into my feet, hands and the roots of my hair.
I see the sun's ball through a mist,
And you, whom my very presence sickens,
I see you in a mist, darkening.
My eyes go dark. Now the light of the sun
Can resume its purity unspoiled.

PANOPE

My lord, she is dying.

THESEUS

If only
The results of her evil could die with her.
Come. Now my error of judgement
Is so monumental and plain
Let us go weep at my son's body.
Let us embrace the little of him that's left
And expiate the madness of my prayer.
We shall give him the honours he has earned.
And to appease his shade,
And in spite of the old crime of your brothers,
Aricia, from today you are my daughter.